Atsushi
Okada
1
NYANKEES

CONTENTS

CHAPTER 1: **HIS NYAME IS...**

NAME'S RYUUSEI.

RYUUSEI, HUH... DUNNO WHAT BACKWATER YOU CAME FROM, BUT HERE IN NEKONAKI TOWN, WE GOT RULES.
AND CRASHING OUR JOINT WITHOUT PERMIS-SION'S OUTTA THE QUESTION.

C'MON! THERE'RE PLENTY OF OTHER PLACES TO HIT UP, NO?
NI (GRIN)

IT'S NOT JUST STUBBORN PRIDE THAT DRIVES THEM TO BRAWL.
YEAH, BUT THIS PLACE IS EXTRA TASTY!
DAMN RIGHT!
Seafood Izakaya uomotsuri
THAT GOOD, HUH? THEN HOW 'BOUT YA HOOK A BROTHER UP!?
HUUUH!?

YOU CAN'T COUNT ON ANYONE IN THIS WORLD—NOT WHEN YOU'RE ONE BAD DAY AWAY FROM DEATH.
WORDS AIN'T WORKIN'!
GET HIM!
OOH!

WHY? WELL, THAT'S 'COS ...
TA (TMP) TA TA TA TA TA
... THESE GUYS ARE...
BIKUU (JOLT)

KITTIES !!

CHAPTER 1 HIS NYAME IS...
...STRAY CATS.
BA (BAM)

COME BAAACK!
DOTA (THUD)
WHOA, WHOA, CUT THAT OUT!
BATA (KATA)
BUT I WANNA PET THE KITTIES!!
BA (HWUP)
NO! THEY'RE DIRTY!!
....
BUT I WANNA !!
TOTE (TMP) TE TE TE

THIS IS
A TALE OF
STREET
CATS
PORTRAYED
AS
HOODLUMS.

FURA (WOBBLE)

FURA

RYUUSEI
MALE DARK TABBY

FURA

FURA

HELL YEAH!

ちゅん

CHUN

MEALTIME, BABY!

ちゅん

CHUN

SU (FUU)
FURI FURI (WIGGLE)
......
DA (LURCH)
SHUBA (FWISH)
!!

GAAAN (SHOCK)
CHIRP! CHIRP!
PATA (FLAP)
TA
TA
TAN (TMP)
HEY! THAT WAS MINE...!!
AW, MAN! IT GOT AWAY!
OOH!!!
???
FEMALE TARGET

MURAA (LOOM)
NICE FACE! SWEET ASS!

PURUN (JIGGLE)
I'M READY TO BUST A NUT!!

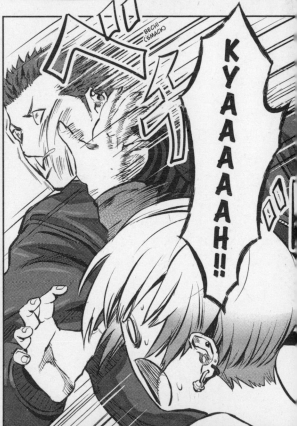

BECHI (SMACK)
KYAAAAAH!!
ZUDE (THUMP)
MRROW!!

THE HELL'S WRONG WITH YOU!?

ZA (FWIP)
......

JUST THOUGHT YOU WERE KINDA CUTE.

EH...
PO (BLUSH)

WHAT DO YOU GO BY?
SU (FWOOP)
...MII.

PERO (LICK)

PERO

PERO

SO, MII-CHAN, WHADDAYA SAY YOU AND ME DO SOME GROOMING?

HUUUH!?

AS IF! WHO ARE YOU ANYWAY!?

BA (YANK)

NAME'S RYUUSEI.
YOU'RE NOT... FROM NEKO-NAKI TOWN, ARE YOU?
NOPE.
WHERE ARE YOU FROM?
A GOOD WAYS AWAY.

JIII (STARE)

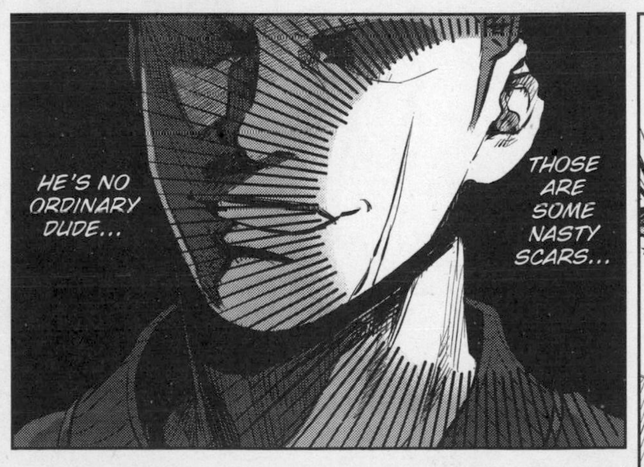

THOSE ARE SOME NASTY SCARS...
HE'S NO ORDINARY DUDE...

SO WHAT BRINGS YOU HERE?
I'M LOOKING FOR A CALICO TOM WITH A SCARRED EYE.
SU (FWIP)
?
A MALE CALICO? THAT'S RARE.
SO YOU DON'T KNOW HIM?
NAH. NEVER SEEN ONE.
BUT HANG ON, YOU...
※CALICO TOMS ARE EXCEEDINGLY UNCOMMON—ONLY ABOUT ONE IN EVERY THIRTY THOUSAND IS MALE.

PROWLING AROUND HERE'S GONNA GET YOU INTO TROUBLE.

NEKO-NAKI'S GOT A BUNCHA STRICT RULES.
ONCE THEY CATCH A PLAYER LIKE YOU, YOU'RE DONE FOR.
OOH.

BABY, BABY.
DAT ASS, THOUGH...

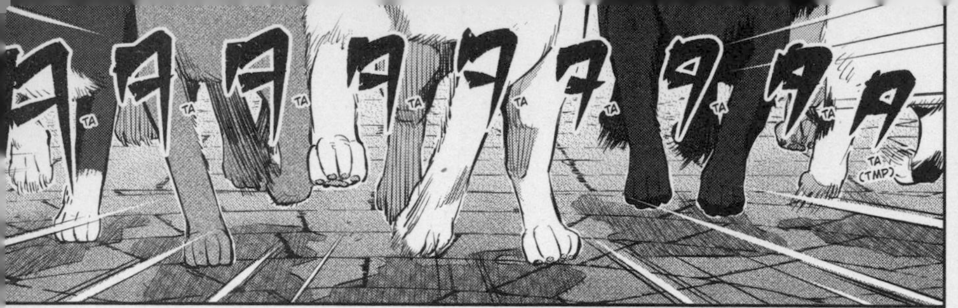
TA
TA
TA
TA
TA
TA
TA
TA
TA (TMP)

THERE HE IS!!
ZA (CROWD)
BASTARD'S HITTING ON MII!

FIRST OUR GRUB AND NOW OUR GAL!?
DON'CHA KNOW THE RULES OF STRAY-CAT SOCIETY!?

WHAT'D I TELL YA?
NOT THAT I CARE.
OH... FROM BACK THERE ...

RULES ...?

WHAT'S THE POINT OF BEING A STRAY IF YOU GOTTA FOLLOW THOSE?

oooooo!!

Y-YOU ...
BUT HEY, HOW 'BOUT SOME OF THOSE BITS !?
I'M STARVING TO DEATH OVER HERE.

DUDE'S STILL MOUTHIN' OFF?
THE FISH IS MINE!
CHILL.

DUNNO HOW THEY DO THINGS IN YOUR FLIMSY CITY...
BA (VWIP)
TCH...IF THAT'S HOW IT IS...
...BUT WE'RE GONNA BEAT THE RULES OF NEKONAKI INTO YA!
SA (SHWP)
IS HE GONNA TAKE ALL OF THEM ALONE!?
SHU (F.WOOSH)

GO (POW)
EAT SHIT!!
BEGO (KAWHAM)
GO TO HELL!!!
DOGO (WHAM)
DOGO
DOGO
GET HIM!!!
DOOON (BAM)
GUH...
SO WEAK!!
SEE THAT!? GUY'S ALL TALK!
GET THAT SMART-ASS OUTTA HERE!

DOSHA
(SPLAT)

EH?
HMM? A CAT?

CAN'T— NEED FOOD...

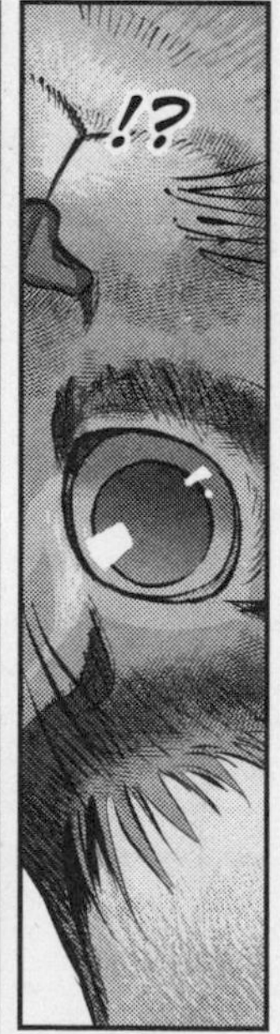
!?

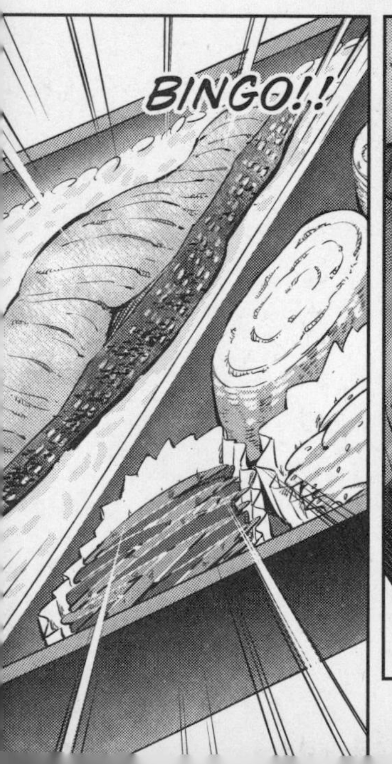
BINGO!!

SU (SHP)
GORO (PURR)
GORO
GORO
GORO
GORO
GORO
GORO
GORO
HM?
GORO GORO GORO
MEOOOW! ♡
GOROOON (PURR)
WH- WHAT'S GOING ON?
OH? WAIT—
HE'S SO CUTE!

WHO'S A GOOD KITTY?
MRROW♡
YES YOU ARE, YES YOU ARE.
MRRROW♡
GUNE (RUB)
GUNE

TH-THAT GUY...

...IS A REAL PRO!

OH, YOU WANT THIS?
FUN (SNIFF)

POTO (PLOP)
MEOW!

GA
GA
GA (MUNCH)
HE'S EATING IT, HE'S EATING IT! ♡

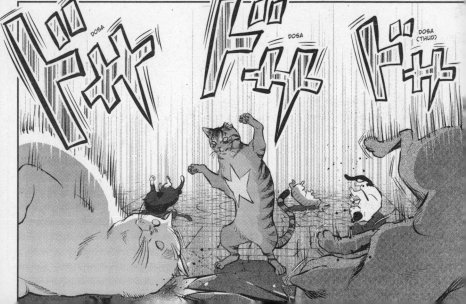

DOSA (THUD)

DOSA

DOSA

PHEW.
I'M FULL AND FINALLY BACK ON TOP OF MY GAME.
ZA (STAND)

N-NO WAY.
HE WAS JUST HUNGRY!?

YORO (WOBBLE)
MRROW...

WHAT'S ALL THIS NOISE?
!!

NOSSHI (THUMP)
DON (BAM)
TAIGA-SAN!!
NOSSHI
TAIGA
MALE ORANGE TABBY

BOSS !!
THAT GUY'S FROM OUTTA TOWN.

BASTARD TRIED EATING OUR FISH, LAID HIS GRUBBY PAWS ON MII, AND EVEN SHOWED HIS TUMMY TO SOME HUMANS!
HE'S ALL OVER THE PLACE!

SU (FUU)

I'M TAIGA, AND I RUN THINGS AROUND HERE.
...WHAT THEY JUST SAID— THAT ALL TRUE?

SURE IS...
THAT A PROB-LEM?

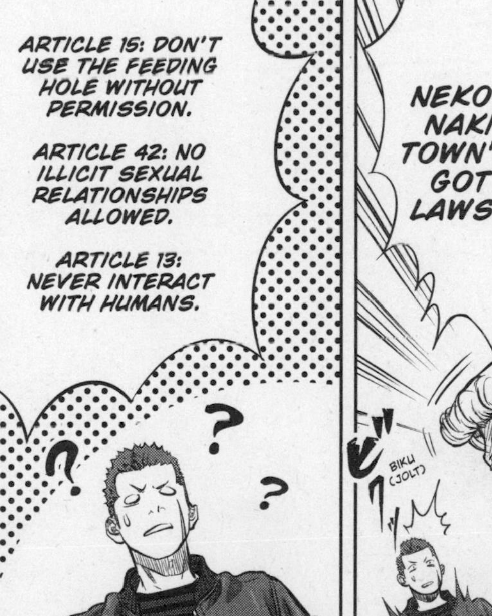
NEKO-NAKI TOWN'S GOT LAWS!
BIKU (JOLT)
ARTICLE 15: DON'T USE THE FEEDING HOLE WITHOUT PERMISSION.
ARTICLE 42: NO ILLICIT SEXUAL RELATIONSHIPS ALLOWED.
ARTICLE 13: NEVER INTERACT WITH HUMANS.

THERE'RE A HUNDRED TOTAL, AND YOU JUST BROKE THREE!!

YOU GOT A HUNDRED OF THOSE DUMB LAWS?

WHAT'D YOU SAY!? YOU BETTER DRILL THE OTHER NINETY-SEVEN INTO THAT SKULL OF YOURS!!

ARTICLE 1: NO LEAVING NEKONAKI TOWN
RTICLE 2: SHO AT DAILY MEETI
RTICLE 3: THOSE 'HO INFRINGE ON HERS' TERRITORY L BE PUNISHED
RTICLE 4: WHEN OUR TERRITORY INFRINGED UPON
ARTICLE 5: IF A FIGHT EVER REAKS OUT, T

ARTICLE 12— HM?

MII-CHAN!

YOU SAW HOW STRONG I WAS, YEAH? YOU FALLING FOR ME YET?

BA (FWIP)

B-BASTARD...

PIKU (TWITCH)

PIKU

YO.

GA (GRAB)

DOGU (POW)

OOF!

GUH...

GU (TUG)

GO (WHAM)

ヨロッ・・・
YORO (SWAY)
GAAH ...!!
DOGA (KAPOW)
I HATE FLIRTY LITTLE LOSERS LIKE YOU...
...MORE THAN ANY-THING !!
GUI (TUG)
LISTEN, PUNK.
DOZA (SKID)

GOT THAT, YOU LITTLE SHIT!!?

GO (WHAP)

GO

GO

THAT'S TAIGA-SAN FOR YOU!

GO

GO

GO

NO MERCY FOR CAT-CALLERS.

IF YOU'VE LEARNED YOUR LESSON, THEN GET LOST ...
...FOOL.
ZA (STEP)

ZUUUN (DOOOOM)

NICE JOB, BOSS!
BOSS! YOU'RE THE BEST!
ZA
ZA

...REAL HARD-ASS, AREN'CHA ?

!?

BUT WHERE D'YOU GET OFF IMPOSING YOUR RULES ON EVERYONE ELSE?
YURA (SWAY)

HUH?
HOW'S HE STANDING BACK UP...!?

IF I SPOT A CUTE MOLLY, I'M MAKING NOISE.

ZA (FWIP)

ZA
IF THERE'S TASTY GRUB, I'M GETTIN' MY FILL.
BA (SWING)
SON OF A —!!
BASHI (CATCH)

GUN
(YANK)
GAAH
!!!

GU (CLENCH)
LIVING FREE IS...
BO (SHOOM)

...WHY I'M ON THE STREET !!!

DOGA
(KAPOW)

DOSA
(THUD)

...WHAT'D... HE JUST SAY!?

B-BOSS!?
TAIGA-SAN!!
ZAWA (CHATTER)

HE TOOK DOWN TAIGA, THE UNDEFEATED TOP CAT...!?

THE POWER BALANCE IN THIS TOWN...
...IS ABOUT TO SHIFT.

ZAN (BAM)
SURE ARE A LOT OF CATS FIGHTING TODAY.
THEY'RE SO CUTE EVEN WHEN THEY FIGHT. ♡
CHAPTER 1 END

NYANKEES

CHAPTER 2

THE BOSS OF NEKONAKI TOWN

......
YOU OKAY, TAIGA-SAN...?

......
ZAN (BAM)
RYUUSEI... JUST WHO ON EARTH WAS THAT GUY?

DUDE TOOK OFF...
WHAT DO YOU THINK HE'S AFTER?
......

MII-CHAN.
ZA (FWIP)

WELL ...
SEE YA.
HUH!?
HANG ON...
WHERE'RE YOU OFF TO!?
MII-CHAN...
SO (CLASP)
......?
GOING'S GONNA BE ROUGH IF YOU CLING TO ME LIKE THAT...
...HUH!?
I'M NOT!
SURE YOU WON'T COME WITH?
NOT A CHANCE!!
'KAY...

WE SHOULD GROOM AND CHILL ONE OF THESE DAYS. ♡
NEVER!!
SHAAA (HISS)
BYE!
AH...

HE BEAT THE BOSS BUT ISN'T PLANNING ON TAKING OVER THIS TOWN?

I'M LOOKING FOR A CALICO TOM WITH A SCARRED EYE.

AFTER SOME CAT, HUH...?

...TAIGA-SAN.

I'LL GO HUNT THE BASTARD DOWN!
ARTICLE 86 SAYS WHEN THE ENEMY RUNS, WE GOTTA DO ALL WE CAN TO—

SHUT IT!!
PYON (HOP)
BIKU (JOLT)
...!!
I LOST TO HIM.
STARTING TODAY, I'M STEPPING DOWN AS BOSS.

OH MY...

HANG ON!
DON'T SAY THAT!
THERE'S GOTTA BE SOME MISTAKE!

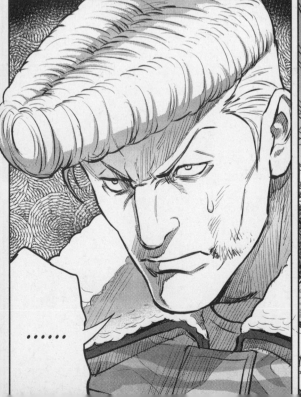

YOU WEREN'T EVEN GOING ALL-OUT AGAINST THAT GUY!

......

GYU (CLENCH)
HE'S STRONG... REAL STRONG...

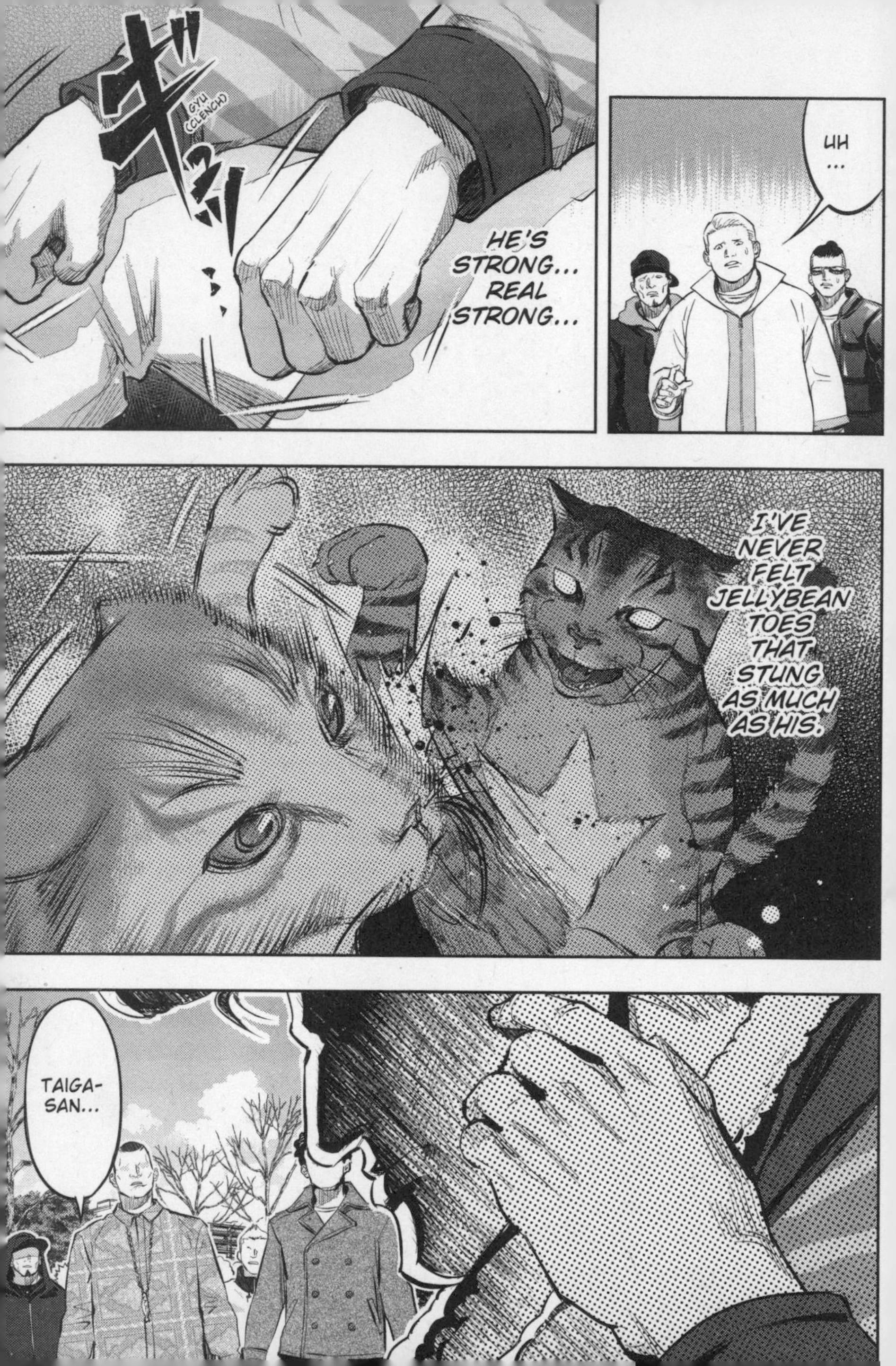

UH ...

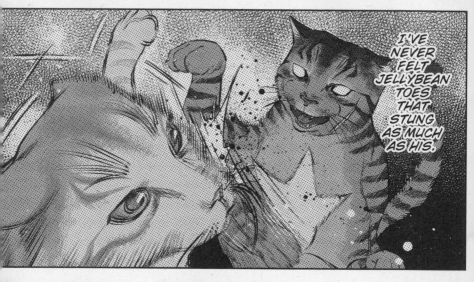

I'VE NEVER FELT JELLYBEAN TOES THAT STUNG AS MUCH AS HIS.

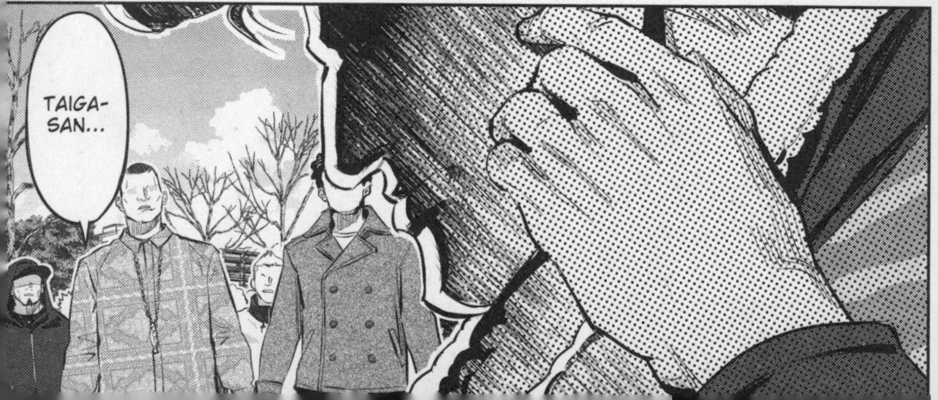
TAIGA-SAN...

BA (BOLT)
WHERE'D HE RUN OFF TO!?
SORRY, WE WERE ALL TOO STUNNED TO CHASE AFTER HIM...
I GOTTA SEE THAT GUY ONE MORE TIME.
FIND HIM...
FIND RYUUSEI!

MM.

NOTHING LIKE...
...A GOOD BOX TO CALM ME DOWN...

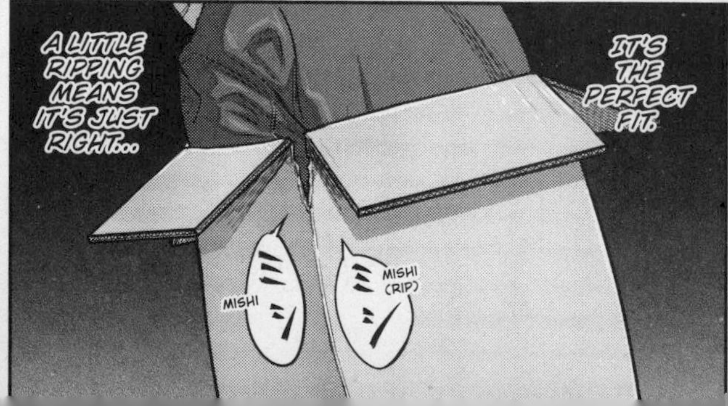
IT'S THE PERFECT FIT.
A LITTLE RIPPING MEANS IT'S JUST RIGHT...
MISHI (RIP)
MISHI

YAAAWN!

ZUPO
(FWP)
MIGHT AS WELL REST UP HERE BEFORE MOVING ON TO THE NEXT TOWN.

MUKU
(POP)
MAYBE IT IS A BIT TOO TIGHT...

ちょこん
CHOKON
(PLOP)

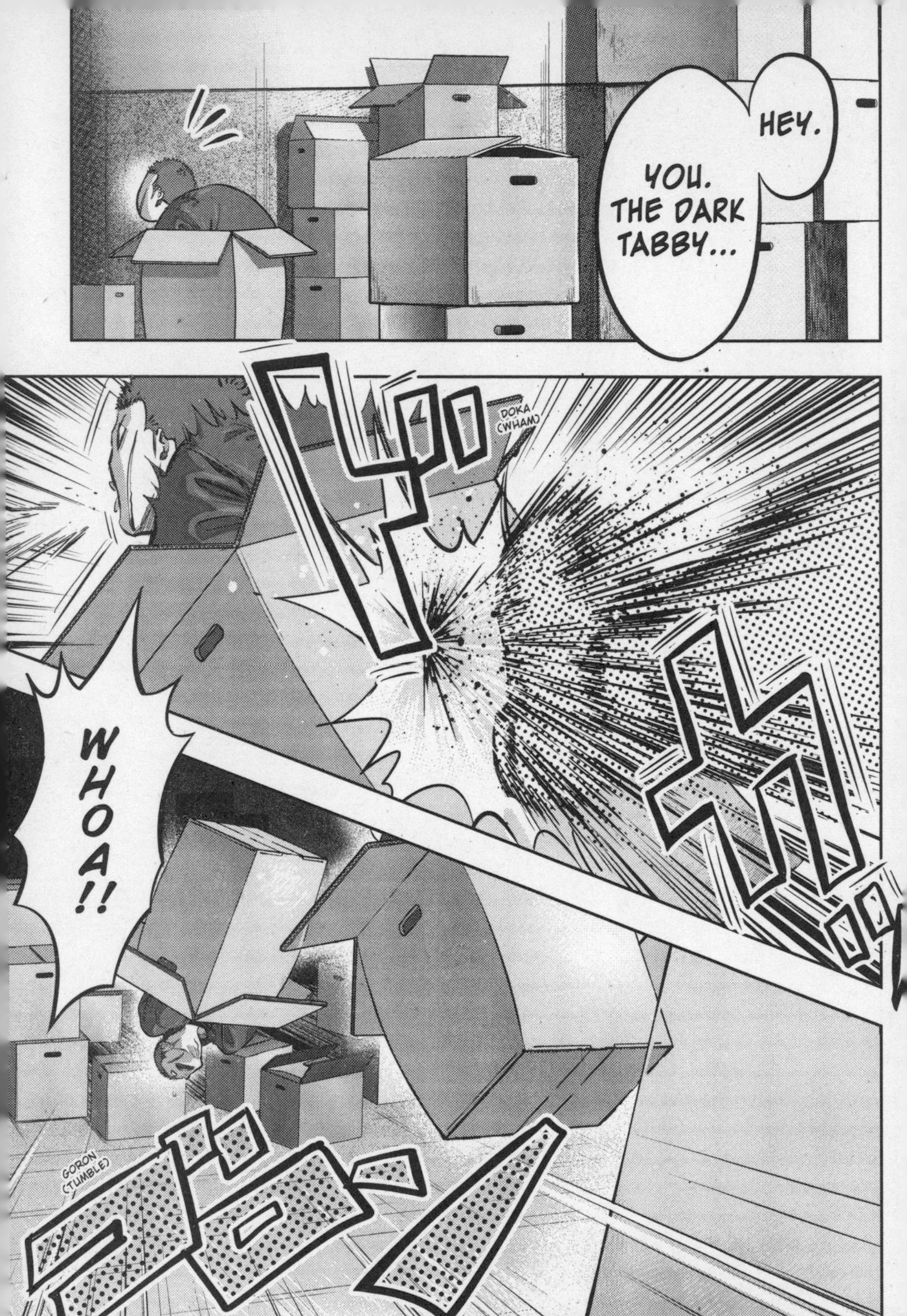
HEY.
YOU. THE DARK TABBY...
DOKA (WHAM)
WHOA!!
GORON (TUMBLE)

BAKO (CRASH)
SA (SLINK)
SA
SU (VWIP)
!?

WHADDAYA THINK YOU'RE DOIN' HERE...?
HMM?
ZUN (BAM)
??? AND ???
MALE TWO-TONES
(LONG-HAIRED)

THE HELL ARE YOU GUYS!?

QUIT PLAYING DUMB...
WE'RE WITH THE "GOBLIN CAT TAILS"—YOUR RIVALS FROM THE NEXT TOWN OVER ...!!

WE'RE THE GANG'S NUMBER TWO DUDES. I'M KINBI.

AND I'M GINBI.

YOU BEST HAVE HEARD OF US...

???
?
?
?
RIVAL GOBLIN WHAT NOW?

NOT SURE WHAT'S GOING ON, BUT MAYBE THEY'RE WHAT'S LEFT OF THAT HARD-ASS ORANGE TABBY'S GANG?

TCH... SOME CATS JUST DON'T LEARN.
BACK FOR ANOTHER BEATING ...?

BA
(THRUST)

GA
(TUG)

I-I CAN'T GET OUT...?
...NO WAY.

MRAAAH!
PYOIN
(BOING)

!?
BITAN
BITAN
BITAN (SPLAT)
BITAN

HMM?

BURU (SHAKE)
HA-HA. CHECK OUT THIS TOOL. HE'S SO SCARED, HE'S TREMBLIN' IN HIS BOX.
BURU

URRRGH...!!
MISHI (RIP)
MISHI

HAH!
DO (POW)
GO (WHAM)
GET OUT!
GA (WHAP)
WAIT.
WAIT!
GA
I SAID WAIT !!
GO
GA

IF YOU THINK THE GOBLIN CAT TAILS ARE GONNA ROLL OVER AND TAKE SHIT, YOU'RE WRONG, BUDDY.
WE'VE GOT A NEW BOSS NOW, AND TIMES ARE CHANGIN'... WHEN WE SPOT SOMEONE FROM A RIVAL CLOWDER, WE MAUL 'EM REAL GOOD.

YOU'VE GOT THE WRONG GUY!! I AIN'T EVEN FROM THIS TOWN!

HUH? THINK YOU CAN FOOL US? NAW. YOU'VE GOT TAIGA'S SCENT ALL OVER YOU...
EH!?
GROSS!

PERO (LICK)
PERO
SESSE (FRET)
SESSE

MEOOOOW!!

BA (FWIP)

RYUSEI!!!

TAIGA!?

'BOUT TIME I FOUND YOU. YOU WERE SKULKING AROUND HERE, HUH? I WAS FOLLOWIN' YOUR SCENT.
ZA (SHUFFLE)
ZA
SU (FUU)

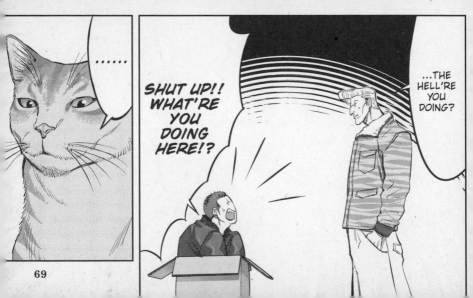

...THE HELL'RE YOU DOING?

SHUT UP!! WHAT'RE YOU DOING HERE!?

......

AS OF TODAY, YOU'RE THE BOSS OF NEKO-NAKI TOWN !!

…HUUUH!?

I SAID I'M HERE TO TURN OVER THE THRONE TO YOU!!
CHAPTER 2 END

CHAPTER 3 GOBLIN CAT TAILS

TCH... DIDN'T THINK TAIGA'D SHOW.

SHOULD WE PULL BACK FOR NOW?

... HMM?

FEH...NO NEED FOR THAT, IT SEEMS.

NIYARI (GRIN)

ニヤッ

TA (TMP)
TA
TA
TA
TA
TA
TA
TA
KINBI-SAN!
DA
DA
DA
DA
DA
DA (STOMP)
GINBI-SAN!

猫鬼の尾

DON (BAM)

GOBLIN CAT TAILS
BATTLE-BASED CLOWDER OF MOSTLY LONG-HAIRED BREEDS

WHOEVER BEATS THE BOSS BECOMES THE NEW BOSS! S'ONLY NATURAL!
LIKE I GIVE A CRAP!!

THEN WHO'RE MY GUYS GONNA LOOK TO!?
AIN'T MY PROBLEM! I'VE GOT MY OWN SHIT TO DEAL WITH!!

BUT ACCORDIN' TO THE RULES—
I DON'T FOLLOW NO RULES!
......

PLAYIN' US FOR FOOLS ...
PURU (SHAKE)
PURU
HEY! LISTEN UP! YOU BETTER NOT UNDER-ESTIMATE THE GOBLIN —

SHAD-DUP !!!

I DON'T GOT TIME FOR YOU PUNKS !
BUZZ OFF!!
...!!

GO (RUMBLE)
GO
GO
TREATIN' US LIKE LI'L PUSSIES ...!!
ZAA (SHWIP)
MESS 'EM UP!!
DA (DASH)

BA (VWIP)
GATA (KLAT)
GATA
HAAAAH!!
BUN (WHIFF)

GUO (SHOOM)
DOGO (KAPOW)
BA (FWOOSH)
EAT THIS!!
GO (POW)
BWUH!

BOGO (WHAM)
HOW'S THAT!?

LOOKS LIKE SOME-ONE'S GETTIN' COZY!!
GYA-HA-HA!
GURA (ROCK)
I CAN'T WIGGLE OUT!!
GURA

DUDE MAKES FOR THE PERFECT TOY!
BOKI (CRACK)
BOKI
PASU (THWACK)
BECHI (SMACK)
PECHI (SLAP)
BESHI
MRRAH MRRAH MRRAH !!!
BESHI (WHAP)
M-M-MRAOW !?

WHAT'S THE DEAL, MAN!?

DOGO (POW)

DOGO

DO

TAN (TMP)

BUWA (ZOOM)

!!

DOGO
(WHAM)
GUN
(SWING)
TO
(THUD)

GO... (SLAM)

TCH!
GA (WHAM)
GO (POW)
HE'S AS STRONG AS WE THOUGHT ...
YO! TAIGA!

WHAT!? YOU TURNING TAIL!?
GO BACK TO YOUR OWN TURF, AND I WON'T HUNT YOU DOWN!!
NAW, LISTEN ...
WE GOT AN OFFER.

HOW 'BOUT YOU JOIN THE GOBLIN CAT TAILS?
!?

HERE'S THE PLAN—
OUR NEW BOSS WANTS TO START A "CAT KINGDOM"...
...AN IDEAL PLACE WHERE BED, FOOD, SAFETY...
...EVERYTHING'S GUARANTEED.

HA-HA-HA...
!
YOU ACTUALLY BELIEVE IN THAT MAKE-BELIEVE SHIT?
AND YOU CALL YOURSELVES STREET CATS!?
US STRAYS ARE NEVER SURE ABOUT OUR NEXT MEAL OR BED.
WE FIGHT FOR OUR LIVES AND OUR TERRITORY.
WE SURVIVE WITHOUT RELYING ON ANYONE!! WITH OUR HEADS HELD HIGH!!

...TCH.
THIS TOWN'S GOT ONE DUMB, HARDHEADED BOSS, HUH...?
WHAT!?
SO BE IT, THEN...

THE GUYS PUTTING UP WITH YOUR SHITTY RULES ARE GONNA COME RUNNING TO US SOONER OR LATER...

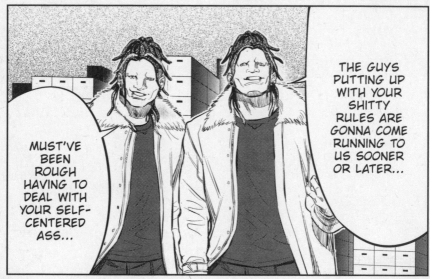

MUST'VE BEEN ROUGH HAVING TO DEAL WITH YOUR SELF-CENTERED ASS...

I DIDN'T MAKE THOSE RULES FOR MYSELF!

THE RULES'RE THERE TO AVOID THE WORST.

I'VE BEEN THERE, SO I KNOW HOW SCREWED UP THINGS CAN GET!

I DON'T WANNA SEE MY PALS IN DANGER, ALL RIGHT!?
...!

JUST KNOW THIS.

I DON'T WANNA SEE YOU GUYS IN DANGER.

......

GU
(SQUEEZE)

NNNGH ...
?

URAAAH!!!
BIRIRI
(RIIIIP)

BARIRII (RIIP)
!?

AHHH! FREE AT LAST...

TH-THE HECK IS THAT CRAZY POWER...?
ALL RIGHT.
IT'S PAW-BACK TIME!
CHAPTER 3 END

NYANKEES

CHAPTER 4 DOUBLE CAT PUNCH

A'IGHT.

WHO'S READY TO GET WHIPPED?

CHOI

CHOI

THIS GUY'S WEAK AS HELL ONE MINUTE, AND A BEAST THE NEXT ...
!
NYARI (GRIN)
TA (TMP)

DOKA (WHAM)
ZUZAAA (SLIDE)
MRROW!!

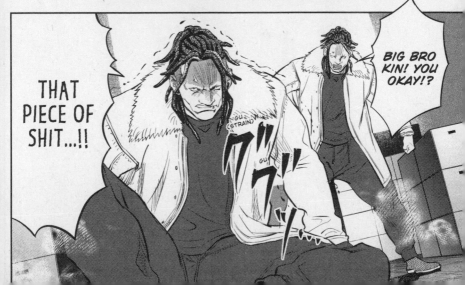

BIG BRO KIN! YOU OKAY!?

THAT PIECE OF SHIT...!!

GU
(STRAIN)

GU

ZAA (VWOOSH)

TEAR 'EM UP!!

SO, ABOUT ME TAGGING IN AS BOSS...

BA (FWIP)

!

YOU FINALLY ON BOARD!?

BUN (WHIFF)
NO!
DOGU (POW)
I'M PASSIN' UP THAT OFFER!
AT FIRST, I THOUGHT YOU WERE A SELFISH, HARD-ASSED MORON.
GAKUN (SLUMP)

BUT ...

...I'M STARTING TO SEE WHY YOUR BOYS GOT ALL THAT RESPECT FOR YOU.

ZUGA (KAPOW)

HA! WHAT'S UP WITH THAT!?

YOU AIN'T OUTTA THE WOODS YET!!

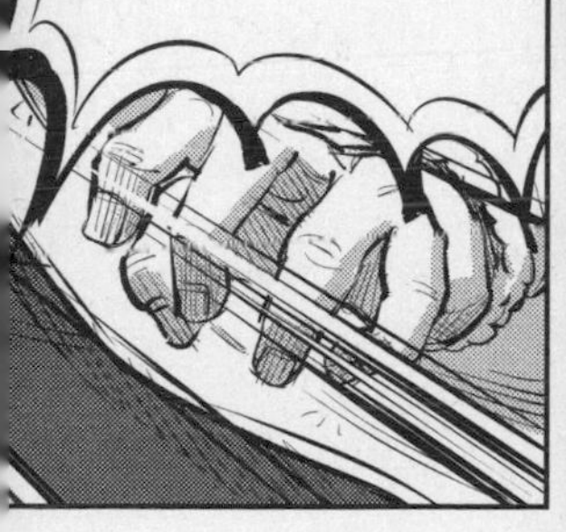

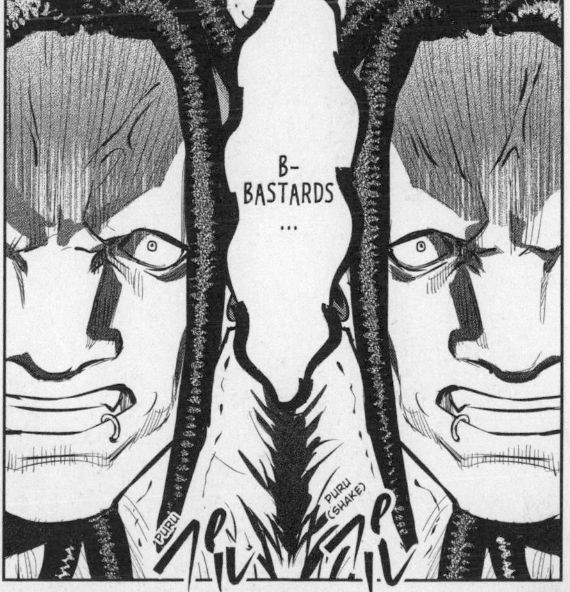
B- BASTARDS ...
PURU (SHAKE)
PURU

DOGO
(BAM)
DO
(WHAM)

HFF!
HFF!
HFF!
HFF!
HFF!

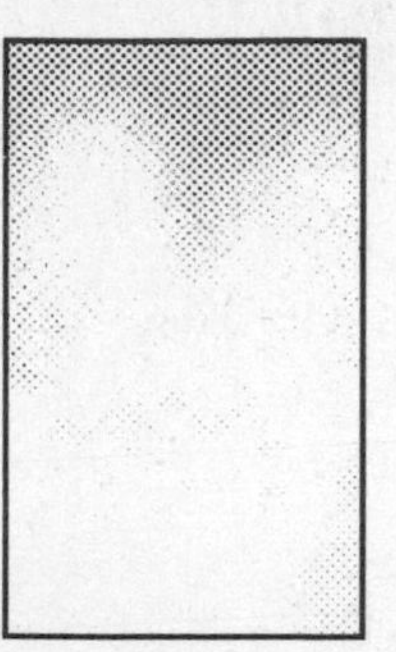

HFF!
NOT BAD FOR AN IDIOT WHO CAME UP WITH A HUNDRED STUPID RULES!
HFF!
HFF!
ZIP IT!

HA-HA...
HEH...

GOTSUN
(BUMP)
ゴツッ

STILL...
THIS FIGHT...IT PROBABLY RILED UP THE GOBLIN TAILS BIG TIME.
THOUGH THEY SURE RAN AWAY FAST.

I KEEP HEARING THAT. "GOBLIN CAT TALES"...
IS IT SOME KINDA STORY ABOUT A MYTHICAL MONSTER?
SOUNDS SCARY.
IT'S THEIR GROUP NAME!

THEY STARTED OUT AS A RIVAL SQUAD FROM THE NEXT TOWN OVER.
WELL, ANY TWO GROUPS SHARING A TURF BORDER ARE GONNA BE AT ODDS...
NEKONAKI TOWN
EVER SINCE THEY GOT THIS NEW BOSS, THOUGH, THEY'VE BEEN WEIRDLY AGGRESSIVE.
TAIGA
猫鬼の尾
NEW BOSS
KINBI, GINBI
NEXT TOWN OVER

NEW BOSS... HUH...
......

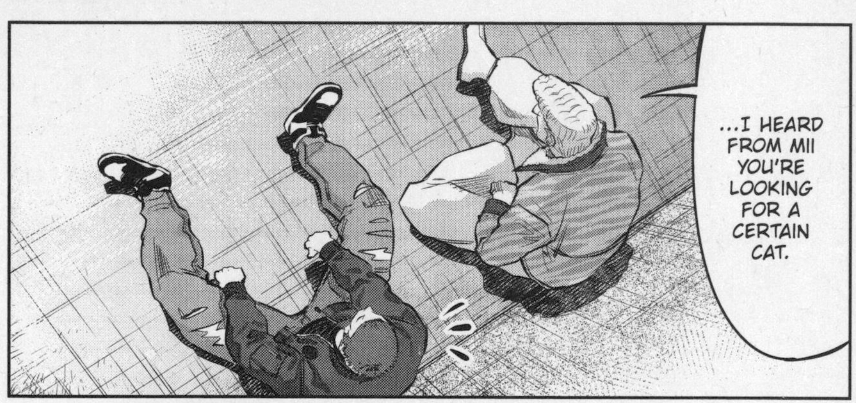
...I HEARD FROM MII YOU'RE LOOKING FOR A CERTAIN CAT.

TRUTH IS, SOMETHING ABOUT THAT JUMPED OUT AT ME.
NOW, THE TAILS' NEW BOSS...I'VE NEVER MET THE GUY, BUT...

...THEY SAY HE AIN'T FROM HERE, AND THAT HE'S GOT A SCARRED EYE.
!?

I GOT A FEELING HE MIGHT JUST BE CONNECTED TO YOUR GUY.
CHAPTER 4 END

NYANKEES

CHAPTER 5 ON A MOONLIT NIGHT...

THE GOBLIN CAT TAILS ARE STARTING TO MAKE TROUBLE.

SO BE
ALERT.

I DON'T WANT ANY OF YOU STEPPIN' A PAW OUTTA OUR TERRITORY ALONE.

GOT IT!
YES, SIR!

BUT ...

...WHAT HAPPENED WITH THE TAILS?
THEIR OLD BOSS WAS STILL STRONG, AND IT'S WEIRD THAT WE HAVEN'T HEARD OF A POWER GRAB.

I WONDER WHAT THE NEW BOSS IS LIKE.
ZAWA (CHATTER)
ZAWA
THAT GANG ALSO GOES BY...
...THE "LONG-HAIRED SQUAD," SO MAYBE THE NEW GUY FITS THE BILL TOO?
...

....

HEY.

YOU'VE BEEN ACTING FUNNY SINCE GETTING BACK... WHAT'S UP?

...YOU KNOW WHERE THE TAILS' HIDEOUT IS?

...WHAT ARE YOU THINKING?

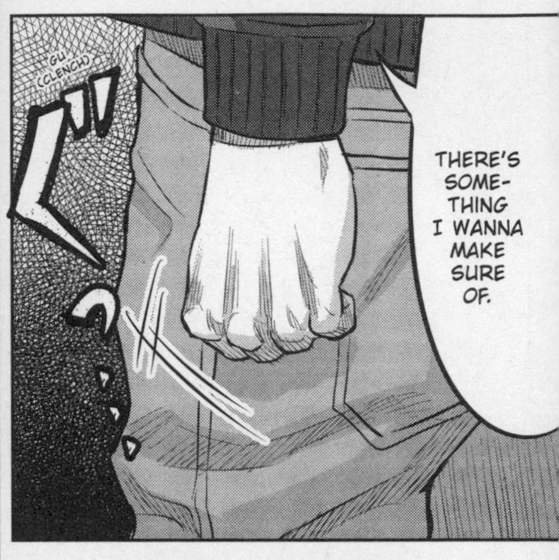

DIDN'T YOU HEAR A WORD TAIGA SAID? THE GOBLIN CAT TAILS RUN A MUCH BIGGER OPERATION THAN US.
THEY'VE GOT AT LEAST TWICE OUR NUMBERS TOTAL.

YOU GOT THAT RIGHT.

AND THERE'S MORE TO THAT JUMP-STARTED GANG THAN JUST ITS NUMBERS.

?

ヒラッ
HIRARI (FWOOP)

スタッ
SUTA (TMP)

MRRRAW...
???
MALE
TORTOISESHELL

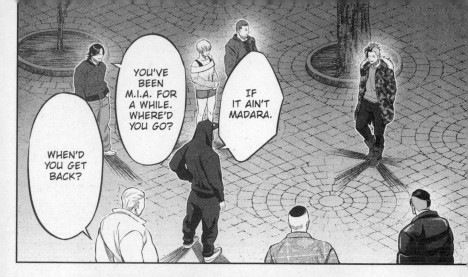

IF IT AIN'T MADARA.
YOU'VE BEEN M.I.A. FOR A WHILE. WHERE'D YOU GO?
WHEN'D YOU GET BACK?

WELL, I HEARD THERE WAS A STRONG NEW CONTENDER ON THE BLOCK.
CHIRA (GLANCE)

...
WORD GETS TO YOU QUICK AS USUAL.

RYUUSEI-SAN, RIGHT? I'M MADARA, THE INFO BROKER.
AH.

MADARA'S YOUR CAT FOR INTEL ON THE BEST JOINTS, CLOWDER ACTIVITY, AND JUST ABOUT ANYTHING IN THE CAT WORLD.

A TORTIE TOM ...!?

HMM ?
OH YEAH. THAT'S ANOTHER RARE COMBO, I GUESS.

ANOTHER UNCOMMON DUDE... THE FIRST I'VE MET BESIDES HIM.

※*LIKE CALICOS, GENETIC FACTORS MAKE MALE TORTOISESHELLS ESPECIALLY RARE.*

ANYWAY, HE'S ALWAYS HANGING AROUND FOR THE LATEST NEWS...
...SO HE DOESN'T COME OFF AS ALL THAT RARE TO US.
HE'S A FREAK WHO'D SOONER JUMP AT INTEL THAN A CHUNK OF FISH.

HEY! THAT'S COLD, MAN!
HA HA HA!

...
MEOW.

THERE'S SOMETHING I WANNA KNOW.

YEAH?

WHAT'S THE GOBLIN CAT TAILS' BOSS LIKE?
...HE A CALICO?

SURE IS.

!

SU (SSK)
...

HEY. RYUUSEI.
I KNOW WHAT YOU'RE THINKING, BUT YOU AIN'T WALTZIN' OVER THERE ALONE.

EVEN A MORON LIKE YOU HAS GOT TO KNOW HOW RISKY IT IS TO GO SOLO INTO ANOTHER CLOWDER'S TERRITORY.
......

MII-CHAN, YOU'RE THAT WORRIED FOR ME...?
HUH?

REST EASY, 'COS I'D NEVER DO ANYTHING TO MAKE YOU SAD.
KIRI (SPARKLE)
HUUUH!?

LIKE I'D WORRY OVER YOU!! ALL OF NEKONAKI TOWN'S AT STAKE HERE!!

MROW!
KERI (THRASH)
KERI
MRAAH!

ANYWAY...

...LET'S CALL IT A DAY. WE'RE ALREADY WORN OUT FROM THE FIGHT.
AT SUNRISE, WE'LL GATHER OUR TROOPS AND MARCH INTO THE TAILS' TERRITORY.

IT'S ABOUT TIME NEKONAKI MET FACE-TO-FACE WITH THIS NEW BOSS.

...RIGHT.

SUTA
SUTA (TMP)
STUPID RYUUSEI. ACTIN' LIKE HE'S HOT STUFF.

WHENEVER THAT CALICO COMES UP, HE GETS ALL BENT OUTTA SHAPE.

KIRI (SPARKLE)
I'D NEVER DO ANYTHING TO MAKE YOU SAD.
IRA (GRR)

ANY CONCERN'S WASTED ON HIM.
SU (SSK)
BA (WHOOSH)
!?

MII'S GONE!?

SHE WAS HERE JUST YESTERDAY, BUT...
ZAWA (CHATTER)
...NOW THERE'S NO SIGN OF HER IN THE PARK...!

MII-
CHAN
...!?

TAIGA-SAN!

I FOUND THIS RIGHT AROUND WHERE SHE USUALLY SLEEPS...

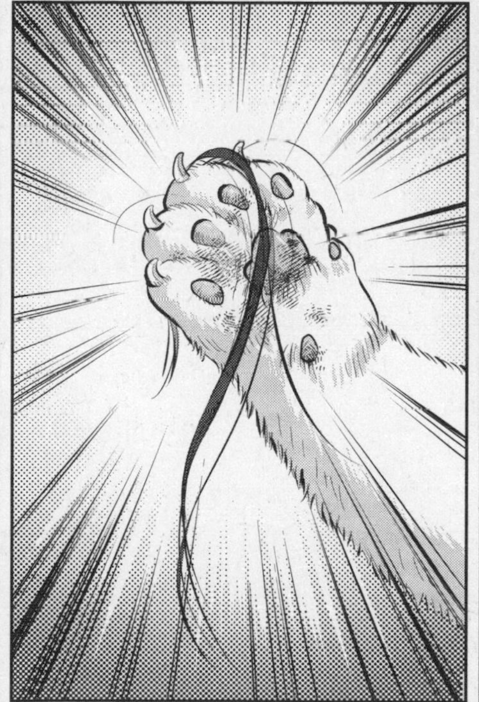

LONG HAIR...

THE GOBLIN CAT TAILS...!!

SOME OF MII'S FUR IS HERE TOO ...
YOU SAYING SHE GOT TAKEN !?

WE'VE SCRAPPED BEFORE BUT ALWAYS MADE SURE TO ABIDE BY THE UNSPOKEN RULES...
BUT STEPPING INTO OUR TURF AND MESSIN' WITH OUR MOLLY...?

DAN (SLAM)

SINCE WHEN DID THEY ABANDON THEIR STRAY-CAT PRIDE!?

MII MIGHT TALK TOUGH, BUT DEEP DOWN, SHE'S A SWEET-HEART.

SHE'S ALWAYS LOOKING AFTER KITTENS WHO LOST THEIR MOMS...

STAY STRONG, MII. WE'LL GET'CHA BACK.
......

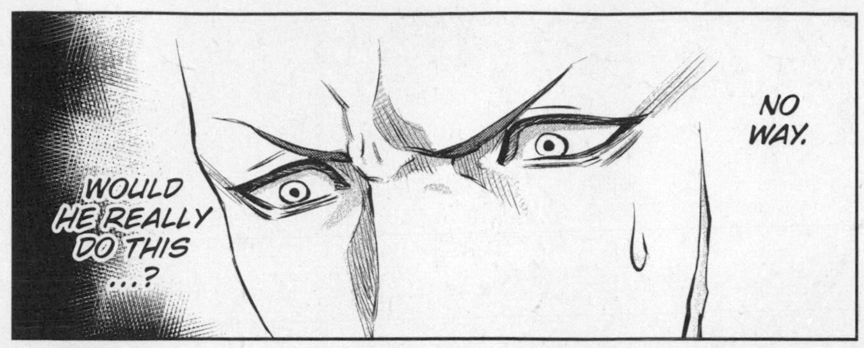
NO WAY.
WOULD HE REALLY DO THIS ...?

RYUUSEI.
ZA (FWIP)

I'M NOT SURE WHAT'S GOING ON BETWEEN YOU AND THAT GUY YOU'RE HUNTING.

BUT IF HE REALLY IS THE TAILS' BOSS, KNOW THAT I WON'T FORGIVE ANYONE WHO MESSES WITH MY PALS.

...I KNOW.

GOOD.
ZA (STEP)

ニャアアッ
WE'RE HITTING UP THE GOBLIN CAT TAILS' HIDEOUT!!

ZUAAA
(BAM)
CHAPTER 5 END

TRANSLATION NOTES

COMMON HONORIFICS

no honorific: Indicates familiarity or closeness; if used without permission or reason, addressing someone in this manner would constitute an insult.
-*san*: The Japanese equivalent of Mr./Mrs./Miss. If a situation calls for politeness, this is the fail-safe honorific.
-*sama*: Conveys great respect; may also indicate that the social status of the speaker is lower than that of the addressee.
-*kun*: Used most often when referring to boys, this indicates affection or familiarity. Occasionally used by older men among their peers, but it may also be used by anyone referring to a person of lower standing.
-*chan*: An affectionate honorific indicating familiarity used mostly in reference to girls; also used in reference to cute persons or animals of either gender.
-*senpai*: A suffix used to address upperclassmen or more experienced coworkers.
-*kouhai*: A suffix used to address underclassmen or less experienced coworkers.
-*sensei*: A respectful term for teachers, artists, or high-level professionals.

PAGE 3

"Fish bits" is known as *sakana no ara* in Japanese. *Sakana* means "fish," and *ara* refers to the head and bony parts of a fish that remain after its meat and organs have been removed. Rather than throwing them away, Japanese people often use these bits in broths and fried dishes due to their juiciness and crunchy texture.

PAGE 4

Nekonaki in Japanese literally translates as a "cat's meow." *Neko* means "cat," while *naki* usually refers to an animal noise or cry.

PAGE 116

In Japanese, the Goblin Cat Tails are referred to as *Byouki no O*, *byouki* meaning "goblin cat" and *O* meaning "tail." Since *byouki* can also be used to describe having an illness, Ryuusei mistakingly thinks Kinbi and Ginbi are referring to a specific ailment affecting their tails.

STOP SCREWING AROUND!!
CHAPTER 6 CALICO
LET ME GO, OR ELSE!!

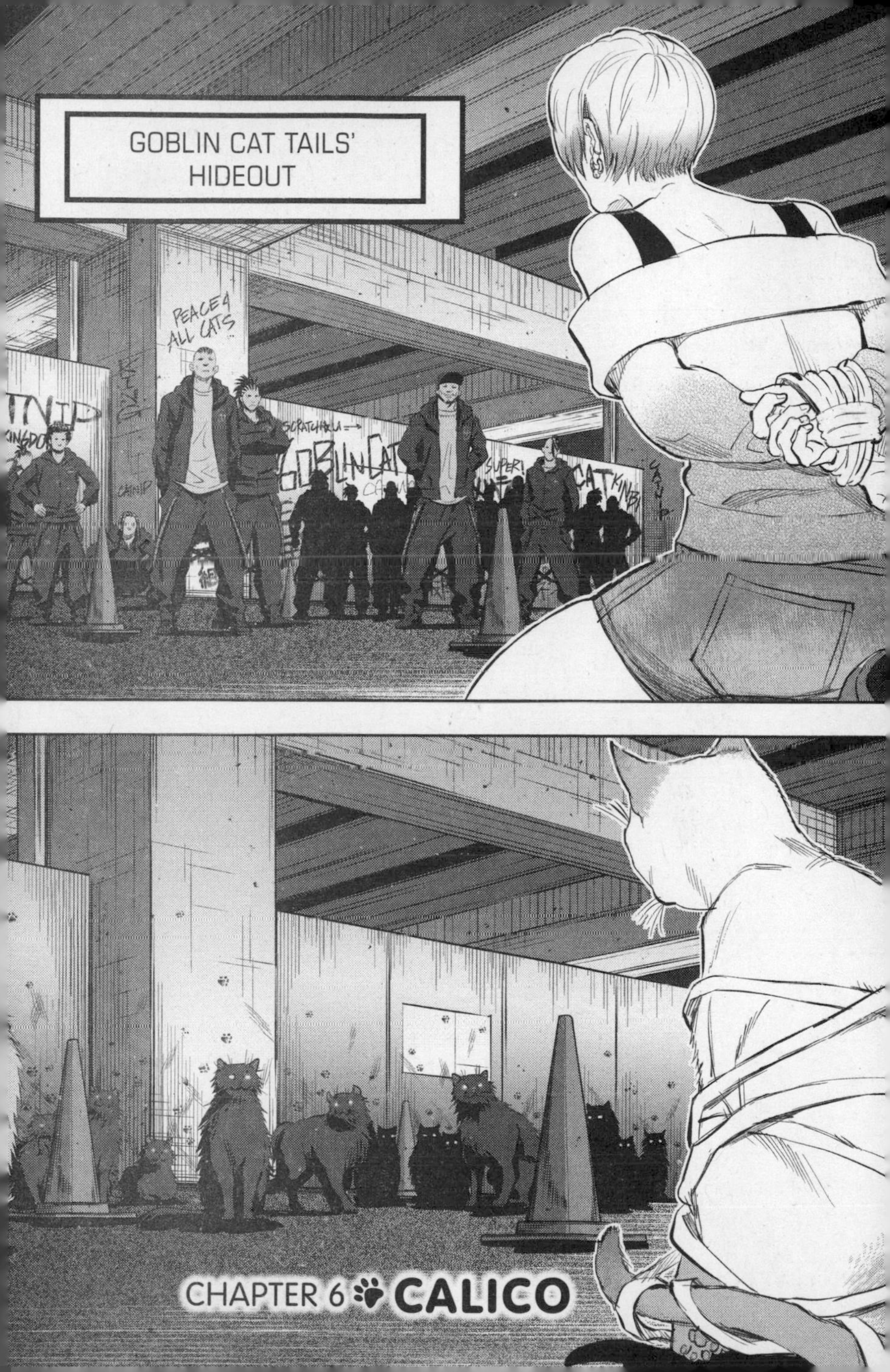

GOBLIN CAT TAILS' HIDEOUT

PEACE 4 ALL CATS

SCRATCHA LA →

GOBLIN CATS

SUPER!

CAT KINGDOM

CHAPTER 6 CALICO

DIDN'T MEAN TO GET ALL ROUGH WITH YOU BACK THERE.
YOU'VE GOT TAIGA AND THE DARK TABBY TO BLAME FOR THAT.

BARI (WHAP) バッ
BARI バッ
GYAAH!
BARI
SHE'S ONE VICIOUS MOLLY, THOUGH.
HIRI (STING) ヒリ
HIRI ヒリ

......
THEIR NEW BOSS... THE CALICO WITH THE SCARRED EYE...
YAAWN.
UTO (SHP)
UTO
KAJI (GNAW)
KAJI
...ISN'T HERE...?

WORD IS THE TAILS GOT A NEW TOP CAT.
KINBI
CATNIP
TAMA WUZ HERE

YEP.
AND WHAT? I'M HERE ON THIS NEW BOSS'S ORDERS? WHAT'S YOUR AIM?

THE BOSS WANTS TO START A KINGDOM... A PARADISE FOR CATS.
BUT FIRST WE GOTTA TAKE OVER EVERY TOWN AND CLOWDER 'ROUND HERE.
CAT KINGDOM
CAT TAILS
CATNIP
KINBI

AS YOU CAN TELL, EVERYONE HERE'S ALREADY ON BOARD.

BUT THAT TAIGA BASTARD DIDN'T WANNA COOPERATE, SO THE BOSS TOLD US TO BRING HIM HERE.

I DO SEE SOME SHORTHAIRS AND GUYS FROM SMALL-TIME CLOWDERS MIXED IN...
HOW'D THIS NEW BOSS GET THEM FOLLOWING ORDERS SO QUICK, THOUGH...?

MRRAAAAH!
BIRI (BZZ)
BIRI
BIRI
BIRI

DOSUN
(FWUMP)

ZA
(STOMP)
ZA

BOSS!!
ZA
ZA

...?

KINBI☆GINB
BOSS.

FC202
CONNOR MEOWGREGOR
GOBLIN CAT TAILS
CATNIP
OSAKA OKADA GANG
IN ORDER TO LURE THE NEKONAKI LOSERS HERE, WE SNATCHED UP ONE OF THEIR MOLLYS.

CHIRA (GLANCE)
...HUH? A MOLLY ...?

OSAKA TAILS
YEAH.
IT'LL BE ENOUGH TO GET THEM COMIN'.

ACK!

GUWA
(LOOM)
GASHI
(GRAB)
GASHI

BUN (SWING)
シャァァァァ

GASHAAAAA (SLAM)
WHO TOLD YOU TO GO AFTER A MOLLY !?
HUUUUUH?!?!?!??

S-S-SORRY!!

SHE JUST HAPPENED TO BE A MOLLY!?

DON'T TELL ME YOU WERE AIMIN' FOR HER FROM THE START!!

W-WE WERE...

... YOU'RE NOT GETTIN' A DAMN THING, ARE YA !?
BURU (TREMBLE)
ブル
SEX, BREED, COLOR, STRENGTH... NONE OF THAT MATTERS IN MY CAT KINGDOM!
BURU
ブル
REAL SORRY.
BURU
ブル
BURU
ブル
猫鬼の尾
......
JI (STARE)
じっ
HEY...
ZA (STOMP)
ザッ

GASHAN
GASHAN (RATTLE)
BA (FWIP)
MII-CHAN!!!
MII!!
!!

DAN (BAM)

WE'RE ALL HERE TO SAVE YOU!!

WHY JUST YOU TWO!?
HERE!!
SOME, UH, STUFF HAPPENED ...
DO DO DO DO DO DO DO DO DO
DO (TMP)
HANG IN THERE, MII.
WE'RE COMING FOR YA.

ワンッ
WOOF!
ワンッ
WOOF!
ワンワンッ
WOOF!
WOOF!
ぴょっ
PYO (BOING)
チョロロロロロ
CHORORORORO (WIGGLE)

バッ
BA (FWIP)
バババッ
BA
BA
BA

Seafood Izakaya Uomatsuri
HMM?
ドドドドドドド
DO (TMP)
DO
DO
DO
DO
DO
DO

Seafood Izakaya Uomatsuri
HEEEY! YOU FELLAS NOT GONNA EAT TODAY?

※THE KIWI PLANT IS RELATED TO CATNIP AND HAS A SIMILAR INTOXICATING EFFECT ON CATS.

HUH!?
SHIIIN (SILENT)
WE'RE ALONE!?

C'MON, REALLY ...?
THEY'LL SHOW UP EVENTU-ALLY...
"RULES" MY ASS ...

ANYWAY!
NO PARKING

MII-CHAN!
YOU'RE NOT HURT !?
PARARI (SWISH)
N-NO.
TAMA WUZ HERE
GINBI

......
SU (FWIP)
BASTARDS.
KINBI RULES!!!

TOOK THE COWARD'S ROUTE 'COS YOU COULDN'T BEAT US, HUH?

AIN'T LIKE THAT, MAN. WE JUST NEEDED TO GET YOU HERE.

I WANNA MEET THIS NEW BOSS.

HAVE A LI'L CHAT.

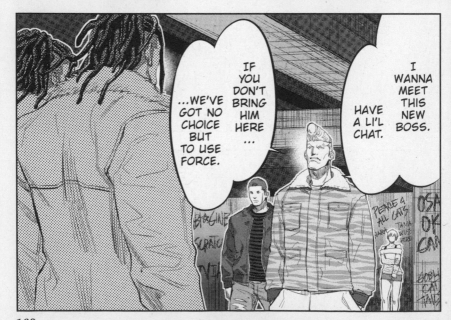

IF YOU DON'T BRING HIM HERE...

...WE'VE GOT NO CHOICE BUT TO USE FORCE.

PEACE 4 ALL CATS

THE NEW BOSS ...!

WHERE IS HE?

ZA (SHUFFLE)

HA.

NO CHOICE BUT TO USE FORCE ...?

ZA

ZUUUUUN (LOOM)
JUST THE TWO OF YOU?
CATNIP
GOBLIN CAT
4LYFE
GINBI
GRILLED FISH
KINBI☆GINBI
MACKEREL♡
NYANKEES
GOBLIN

MOVE
...

DOKUN
(BADUMP)
BOSS
...

DOKUN
(BADUMP)
CALICO...

SCARRED EYE...
DOKUN

YOU
...!!
CHAPTER 6 END

★ ★ ★

PRODUCED BY:

Special Thanks

PICCHI

CHIBI

Atsushi Okada

Translation: Caleb Cook

Lettering: Rochelle Gancio

Yen Press
1290 Avenue of the Americas
New York, NY 10104

Visit us at yenpress.com
facebook.com/yenpress
twitter.com/yenpress
yenpress.tumblr.com
instagram.com/yenpress

First Yen Press Edition: January 2019

Yen Press is an imprint of Yen Press, LLC.
The Yen Press name and logo are trademarks of Yen Press, LLC.

The publisher is not responsible for websites (or their content) that are not owned by the publisher.

Library of Congress Control Number: 2018958637

ISBNs: 978-1-9753-8337-4 (paperback)
978-1-9753-8338-1 (ebook)

10 9 8 7 6 5 4 3 2 1

WOR

Printed in the United States of America